POEMS TO **SHOUT OUT LOUD**
AND SOME TO *Whisper*

by Ernest Henry

These are poems for **SAYING OUT LOUD**
to each other.

At home, on the bus, in the bath, at school, behind the

dustbins or while you are watching telly. Live them **LOUD**

Some are silly

Some are sad

Some are whatever you want them to be.

CONTENTS
Poems to Shout out Loud

Poems to SHOUT out LOUD

NORTHBOROUGH PRIMARY SCHOOL
CHURCH STREET
NORTHBOROUGH
PETERBOROUGH PE9 9BN
01733 252204

"This is dedicated."
"What? dedicated?"
"Yes. Dedicated to –"
"Te-rr-i-ff-i-c!"
"Please don't interupt."

"SOR - RY!"

"DE-*DI*-CA-*TED*
DE-*DI*-CA-*TED*"

"Will you *pleeeaasse* be quiet!"
"Sorry."

"De-*di*-ca-*ted*, de-*di*-ca-*ted*"

"- to my two sons,
Nicholas and Rupert -"

"Yeah!!!!!"

"Shhhh"
"Sorry"
"-tomytwosonsNicholasandRupertwithoutwhomthisbookwouldneverhavebeeninspired."
"You finished now???"
"Yes. Thank you."
"Good."
"DE-*DI*-CA-*TED*, DE-*DI*-CA-*TED*, DE-*DI*-CA-*TED*, DE-*DI* -"

First Published in Great Britain in 1996
Bloomsbury Publishing Plc, 2 Soho Square, London W1V 6HB

Copyright © Text Ernest Henry 1996
Copyright © Illustrations Paul Daviz 1996

The moral right of the author has been asserted
The moral right of the illustrator has been asserted
A CIP catalogue record of this book is available from the British Library

ISBN 0 7475 2524 2

Printed by Cox and Wyman Ltd, Reading Berkshire

10 9 8 7 6 5 4 3 2 1

Poems to
SHOUT
out Loud

SEA SNAIL

I'm a big fat sea snail
Sitting on the rocks
And when people pass me by
I can see their socks.

"BEN, BEN" . . .

Ben, Ben had a face like a hen
And a mouth in a shape of an "O"
Two ears like an ellie,
A big fat belly,
And a voice with a sound of a crow!

His body was scrawny,
His hair was tawny,
His nose dripped goo like a tap.
His skin was spotty,
And right on his botty
Was a boil as big as a bap.

With clothes all wrinkled,
His tie was sprinkled
With food which
 dripped from his chin.

But the point of this story,
His crowning glory
Was that Ben had a
 beautiful grin!

THE 'ORRIBLE

"Come 'ere you 'orrible little boy," said the 'orrible dirty old pirate.

"Come 'ere and sit on my knee and I'll tell you a frightening old sea story about 'orrible pirates like me."

But the 'orrible little boy just looked up at the pirate and grinned, his teeth all shiny white against his dirty face.

"Yeah, come 'ere you 'orrible little boy," screeched the 'orrible old pirate's equally 'orrible old parrot, perching on the pirate's dirty old shoulder. "Come 'ere and sit on his knee and he'll tell you a story."

The 'orrible little boy climbed on to the pirate's knee. But instead of listening to a story, he grabbed one of the parrot's legs and pulled it off!

"You 'orrible little boy!" screeched the parrot, his eyes nearly popping out of his head. "You pulled my leg off."

HHHHHHHHH

(a dropped aitch!)

4

LITTLE BOY

But the little boy just grinned, his teeth all shiny white against his dirty face and he threw the parrot's leg over his shoulder.

"What a 'orrible little boy," exclaimed the pirate in amazement, but the little boy just stuck a finger into his right nostril, wiggled it about, pulled it out and wiped it all down the pirate's tatty waistcoat.

"What a 'orrible little boy," screeched the parrot, amazed at the vileness of the boy.

But the boy grabbed the poor parrot and pulled his remaining leg off. Whereupon the parrot bounced from the pirate's dirty old shoulder, on to the floor to the pirate's dirty old boots, followed swiftly by his erstwhile leg which was thrown on to the floor by the 'orrible little boy.

"What a terrible thing to do," said the old pirate in pure amazement. "Yes, a terrible thing," came the parrot's voice from the floor, at the pirate's feet.

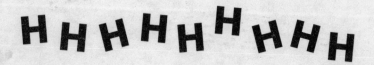

But the 'orrible little boy just grinned, his teeth all shiny white against his dirty face, and stuck a finger into his left nostril, wiggled it about, pulled it out and wiped it all over the pirate's tatty old waistcoat. Then the boy got off the pirate's knee, turned, waved goodbye and walked on home.

"What a 'orrible little boy," said the pirate.

"Yes, 'orrible," squawked the poor parrot, lying on his side on the floor.

THE STORY OF EDMUND PO

This is the story of Edmund Po
Whose reputation followed wherever he'd go.
A strange looking child,
Gangly and gorn,
Apparently this was the way he was born.

His clothes were rumpled
His hair lay flat.
Specs of dandruff rimmed his hat
And his shoulders (such as they were).

And of great notice and particular piff:
Edmund Po would perpetually sniff.
And sniff he would from his rather long honker:
In all it must be said
He was a bit of a plonker.

But –

Edmund Po was his school's greatest hit
Because the lad knew how to spit.
And spit he did and spit he could:
He'd spit from Richmond to Boreham Wood.

The art of spitting was his life's ambition
In that he carried on a family tradition
Started by his Great Aunt Ceel
Who managed a spit from Calais to Deal.

Anyway –

News of Po leaked through the school gate
To the World of the Media and the Good and the Great.
And soon, very soon, wherever he'd go
A trail of newsmen would follow their Po:

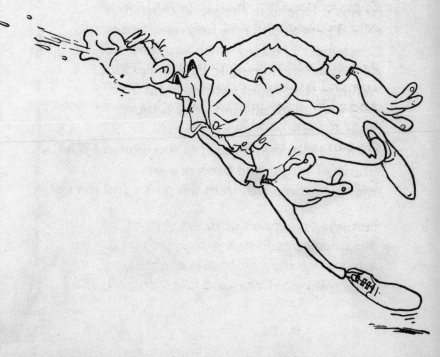

They'd follow him up, they'd follow him down,
From here to there – all over Town.
And as a result of this tremendous fame
Po'd become a household name.

You saw him in chat shows all day long,
Someone even wrote a song.
"We know Po,
We know Po"
People would chant wherever they'd go!
And Po things were bought, whatever the cost.
He even had breakfast with David Frost.

Yes –

Po was a legend in the world of sports,
He did pantos and telly and news reports.
Contenders lined up which was very nice
He was even challenged by Anneka Rice.
Wembley, Las Vegas, wherever he'd go,
He'd beat them all, and what a show:
Laser lights would pick up his spit
From the moment he spat to the moment it hit
Whatever target had been pre-set.
And Po became rich from the purse and the bet.

His managers gloated and preened with joy
Filling their pockets from the winnings their boy
Was able to earn them. Oh what a time:
Everything rosy – all sublime.

But –

Then one morning Po awoke
His mouth was dry. He drank a Coke.
But still it remained like the desert sands:
Dry as a bone, his saliva glands
Had given up providing Po what he needed
And instead of helping him, now impeded
And actually stopped Po's career in its track
And turned Po into a sporting hack
Commentating every Saturday
On the popular sport's state of play.

But Po's very happy and always a hit
On Celebrity Squares . . . and all from spit!

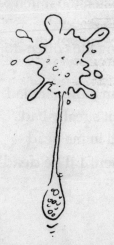

THE DOC

"Open your mouth," said the Doc to the boy
As he prodded around with a flat wooden toy.
"Say Ah! Cough! Ninety-nine!
Well, you're all right. Look just fine!"

"But Doc, I got a real bad pain,"
The boy implored the Doc again.
"It's here, and here, and sometimes there:
It comes and goes, I don't know where."

"It's in your *mind*," said the Great Physician
As he turned the boy round to another position
From which he could observe the little twit
Who'd probably eaten too much Kit
Kat and chocolaty goo –
The way that young kids often do.

"S'not," retorted an indignant lad.
"I can feel it now, it's really bad:
It's on me toes and in me head –
I think in a moment I'll be dead!"

AHHHHHHHHHH

D o c

A wistful lingering, longing look
Came over the Doc as he shook
The glass thermometer from north to south
Before shoving it in his patient's mouth.

"Ninety-eight point six," Doc intoned with delight
As he withdrew the thingie from the little blight-
Er's mouth, and gazed intently at the mercury scale
Which measured temperature and without fail
Gave an accurate report
Of the state of health of the little wart.

"There's nothing wrong with you," the Doc declared
To the wittering loon who persistently dared
To contradict the Diagnosis
Undertaken From Head To Toesis.

And with that the Doc strode to the door,
Told the lad not to be a bore
That he was well enough to go
On the school run in the snow
And not to be such a whimpish pud:
The freezing sleet would do him good.

Doc peered across his waiting room
Filled with sullen lads from whom
He knew he'd get similar tales
Of aches and pains and desperate ails
Contrived to play upon his feelings
Hardened by the years of dealings
With medicine, discipline, rights and Rule
And the strange inhabitants of English School.

"Go, go you malingering lot,"
Doc bellowed to the boys who'd not
Yet realised that their mournful tears
And Tales Of Sick would fall on ears
Deafened by the years of Position
Suffered by the School Physician.

. . . And when they'd gone and closed the door,
Doc had a fit — and fell dead on the floor.

GETTING DRESSED

"What's he doing?" Gerbie said,
As Dad put on his socks and knickers,
Shirt and tie and shoes by Trickers.

"Getting dressed in front of us,"
Nera replied, "and what a fuss.
Never seen anything like it before:
Knobbly knees and rounded tum,
Spindly legs and wobbly bum.
Oh, what a sight,
I've got to lie down.
Bring me a nut, bring me a crumb.
It's all too much and too early too –
What a terrible thing to do!"

"And terribly boring," Gerbie went on
"To have to put on those uncomfortable clothes,
To cover your body from head to toes,
I wouldn't do it. I wouldn't dare:
Gerbils would notice, Gerbils would stare."
"Fancy you in cowboy gear,"
Nera smiled from ear to ear.
"Ten-gallon hat, spur and boot.
Oh what a laugh, oh what a hoot.
Much more interesting than hats and coats!"

And with that the gerbils returned to their oats.

BOBBY THE BOGEY

I'm Bobby The Bogey
I live in yer nose.
If you wriggle yer finger
You'll tickle me toes.
DON'T prod and gauge and dig me out
Leave me peacefully in yer snout.

And DON'T excavate, pick, roll or flick,
That's so disgusting: makes people sick.

Blowwww me gracefully into your tissue –
Don't look at me! What's not at issue
Is how I look lying there:
You shouldn't know. You shouldn't care.
It's private!

Just scrunch up the tissue,
Throw it away.
And like magic I'll return
The following day.

IT'S YOU!!

"It's *You!*" the majestically pompous Voice thundered
As the Hand and its Finger wandered
And alighted upon the oik
As he started to get on his boik.

"Eh?" the oik replied
Looking vacantly from side to side.
"It's *You!*" the Beneficence repeated.
"What's me and why? What have I done?"
The oik was defeated
By who
Kept saying, "It's *You!*"

"It's *You!* you numbskulled twit,"
The Hand's Voice started to spit,
"It's *You!*" it screamed and began to yell,
"It's *You!* For goodness sake someone tell
Him this isn't a joke, this isn't a fix
He's won the lot – he's got all six!"

"Don't you come on like that," the oik retorted.
"Who do you think you are? I'll have you reported,
Floating around the sky
Pointing at anyone passing by.
You could've scared me half to death.
You're drunk – let me smell your breath."

"But it's you, it's you – the Voice now a squeak,
Its Hand shaking and quivering with pique.
"I've chosen you from all the zillions
To win this week's eighteen millions!"

"You can't palm me off with hand-outs,
And anyway, how do I know where you got that money?
There's something fishy, there's something funny
About all this stuff.
I've had enough."

And with that the oik
Got on his boik.

Poems to

RRROOOO

around your

TTTTOOO

SLEEP

Z
Z
Z
Z

Isn't it funny the way people sleep,
Some in a ball, some in a heap.
Sprawled on the bed, with mouth open wide,
Or neatly turning from side to side.

Buried in pillows and covers except
For a leg or an arm which appears from the depth.
Lying on top, flat on the back,
Spinning all night, so by morning prac-

Tically all the sheets and duvets and things
Are tied in a knot till the alarm bell rings.
Some people lie still, but noisily roar
All through the night, perfecting their snore.

There are those I am told who whistle at night;
Mumblers and jumblers and grumblers. And light
Sleepers who wake at the smallest of sounds
And listen for hours as the house groans around.

Lawyers who sleep in their briefs 'stead of 'jamas,
And the restless antics of animal farmers
Who bellow and bawl at their dream-state cows,
Horses, sheep, chickens and sows.

Z
Z
Z
Z
Z
Z
Z

Doctors mumble
"ninety-nine,
Cough, spit, you're
looking fine."
Members of
Parliament bay
and snort,

Swimmers practise their favourite sport
While knocking things off the bedside table:
Lamps, phone, or ghostly fable.

Conductors conduct with pillow and sheet,
Detectives detect but they're more discreet
And only move when no one's looking.
Chefs dream their finest cooking

And with hands flaying around in the air
They rip out a handful of their wife's lovely hair
Thinking it's a bunch of fresh growing parsley –
And what happens next is perfectly ghastly.

The athlete who wakes in a heap by his bed.
And those who rest still, as if they were dead.
But whatever the way, whether lightly or deep,
There's nothing like a good night's sleep.

THE BUSY BEE

I'm busy in the flowers, and I'm busy in the trees.
I'm such a busy body, I'm such a busy bee.
I'm busy making honey, and I'm buzzing busily.
I'm dizzy being busy, I'm busy being me.

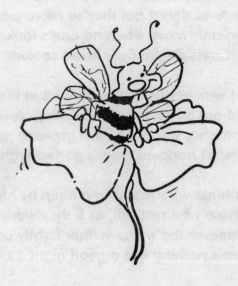

ODD BALL

"I'm a Odd Ball.
A Odd Ball.
A ugly, mugly, pugly, smugly
Odd Ball.

"I lie around the garden shed
Scuffed and scarred. And 'ere instead
Of pretty seams I've got this fread.
A Odd Ball.
A Odd Ball.
A ugly, mugly, pugly, smugly
Odd Ball.

"No one 'ere kicks me around.
I'm tough and strong and make a sound
Like that (x) when I hit the ground,
A Odd Ball.
A Odd Ball.
A ugly, mugly, pugly, smugly
Odd Ball.

"No one plays around with me.
I don't care – I can't see
The point of having fun, I'll be
A Odd Ball.
A Odd Ball.
A ugly, mugly, pugly, smugly
Odd Ball."

SUMA THE PUMA

I'm Suma the Puma from India
I'm the sleekest cat I know –
From Bollywood to Hollywood they call me
To appear on TV show.
I used to go hunting for Sultans –
A family tradition, it's said.
But nowadays I'd rather
Leave that for my Father
And eat sultanas in bed.

I bathe twice a day in warm water
And sharpen my claws with pride,
'Cause every fat cat's daughter
Wants to be my bride.
But I'm tired of the fast track of living.
I'd like something simple instead.
Like watching TV
In the shade of a tree
Or eating sultanas in bed!

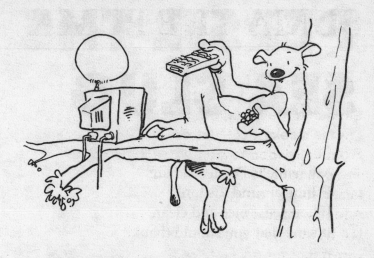

They drag me from Bombay to LA
And although it's a bit of a trip.
I'd rather be home in the jungle
With a mango cocktail to sip –
"To Hurry One's Curry Isn't Clever,"
As the great wise one said.
So I'll take his advice
And stay where it's nice
And eat sultanas in bed!

PERSIL THE SEA SLUG

My name is Persil Sea Slug,
I slime around the tank.
If you see it nice and clean,
It's me that you should thank.

I slurp around and clean the sides
And hoover up the muck,
And if I get an algae break,
I think that I'm in luck.

I chase around the fishes,
I scuttle like a mouse.
I never stop for holidays,
I'm always cleaning house.

I tidy up the shells
And put the seaweed back in
place.
One day I'll catch a little fish
And clean his dirty face.

KING FLORENCE O' DE NILE

In a little inlet
On the Southern coast of France
King Florence o' de Nile stood standing guard.

He got quite sick of people
Rushing by his little house.
He decided the road in front should now be
barred.

So he set up a toll booth
Right beside his garage door,
And another one just by his garden gate.

He stuck a flag upon the roof,
And stood there quite aloof
In the middle of his little Sovereign State.

He charged ten francs for passing by
And five for coming back.
You had to pull the toll bell every time.

Not pulling on the toll bell,
Really just an old bell,
Became the Sovereign State's only crime.

Visitors who didn't have
The right amount of cash
Were given change in Coin of the Realm.

And people came from miles around
To see the little State
And the man who stood so proudly at its helm.

"I'm on to something very big,"
King Flo soon realised
As the money started rolling in quite fast.

"I could be making more dough
If the passers-by-the-door know
They can do a whole lot more than whiz on past."

Queen Jocelyn had the bright idea:
"Give 'em Moules and Frites.
And charge them extra francs to see the view.

"Twenty francs a can of Coke,
Eight for cups of tea,
And ten francs if they want to use the loo."

"Crepes suzettes!" the King declared,
Jumping up and down
As he hugged his Queen and gave her sploggie kisses.

"Sacré Bleu and Ooh la la!
We're rich. I'll buy a crown."
And he did a little dance with his missus.
"We'll start a bank, the Bank of Franc,
And issue stamps and bonds,"
King Flo went on over morning coffee.

"Souvenirs and flags,
T-shirts, caps and bags,
And slabs of King Florence's home-made toffee."

Claude the surly gardener
And keeper of the toll
Complained about the daily growth of work.

From six in the morning
Till fairly late at night
The ringing of the bell drove him berserk.

The pace of life was faster
Than the King had ever thought
As his house became a major tourist spot.

And although the people tolled in
Meant the money rolled in
The King became unhappy with his lot.

"What are we to do?"
He asked Queen Jocelyn
As they sat together counting all their loot.

"We may have lots of lolly
But life is not too jolly
And now there's all this work to do, to boot!

"I have no time to sit and chat,
To take a glass of wine
Or paddle in the sea the way I did:

"The tourists and their cars,
Celebrities and stars –
Is it really worth the extra quid?"

"Give it up," the Queen replied,
"We'll open up the road
And turn it back the way it used to be."

And so they did, and once again
People rush on by
But King Flo has time to paddle in the sea!

Poems with Strange Words to

CHEW

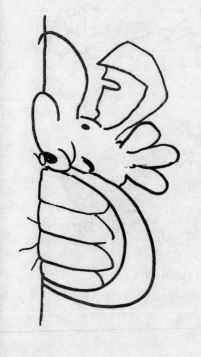

MARIE

Marie, Marie,
M
A
R
I
E.
Has a heart as big as a bus.
She hustles and bustles
And fussels and skittles and
Scuttles around after us.

She prittles and prattles,
Cickles and cackles
About all the gossip she's heard.
You tell her your news
And with eee's, aaah's and oouu's
She'll promise to say "not a word!"

She'll launch into giggledom
Writhing in wiggledom
Darting around like a mouse.
Then with coughing and wheezing,
Much biscuits and teasing
She'll fruntle all over the house.

THE FRENCH DINOSAUR

There was a little dinosaur
Who lived in Southern France.
He liked baguettes and garlic,
And often used to dance.

But when he was confronted
By any kind of foe
He'd raise shoulders up and down
And roar *Hoho, hoho!*

He rolled his r's and drank his wine
And snoozed from twelve to three.
He rumbled round the countryside
In a battered 2CV.

Whenever he got angry
People used to know:
'Cause he'd raise his shoulders up and down
And roar *Hoho, hoho!*

Rrrr – he'd roar from time to time
In an accent thickly French.
Rrrr – he'd roar especially when
He hadn't had his lench.

Rrrr – gesticulating:
He put on quite a show
When he'd raise his shoulders up and down
And roar *Hoho, hoho!*

KING 'AROLD OF EYE

Another 'Orrible Story

There once was a king called King 'Arold of Eye. He was a 'orrible little King famous for his temper which was as 'orrible as he was. The slightest provocation, the merest hint of anyone not doing as he wanted, would send little King 'Arold off into a fierce fizzy rage.

His mum, Queen Fafel, was as beautiful and kind as King 'Arold was 'orrible. She tried and tried to make King 'Arold a nice King, a kind King, a friendly King, but all in vain.

Food was the problem, of course. Queen Fafel wanted King 'Arold to eat good food, nutritious food. But King 'Arold only wanted to eat surgary, gooey, doughy stuff. Which he liked. But which made him nervous and 'orrible.

She tried, pleaded, begged and implored. But nothing worked.

Poor Queen Fafel. She became so sad she strolled around the beautiful gardens of her palace in Eye and wondered what on earth she was going to do.

HHHHHHHHH

(a dropped aitch!)

To take her mind off 'orrible 'Arold, she started to tend and look after part of her gardens and decided to turn one particularly nice bit of it into a lovely vegetable garden.

Every day, she'd leave the palace after brekky, and trundle across the lawns past the peacocks and the lake to her veggie patch. And there she stayed, all day, looking after her lettuces and tomatoes, potatoes and onions, runner beans and peas, radishes and cucumbers, and so many herbs she lost track.

Around the vegetable garden, there were apple trees and pear trees, plum trees, a fig tree and even a vine.

It was a lovely place, Queen Fafel thought, a peaceful place.

King 'Arold was not lovely or peaceful, however! Especially one day after arriving home from school.

Talk about a fizzy mood!

Talk about a raging wozza!

Talk about 'orrible as 'orse manure!

King 'Arold came storming into the Palace.

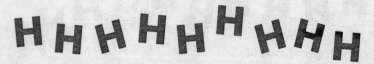

"Where's my tea?" he yelled as he stamped on the cat.

"Where's my tea?" as he threw his crown on the lovely hall table with beautifully arranged flowers, knocking them over and creating a terrible mess all over the place.

"I'm hungry and I need food. And I need it now!"

And he stomped into the kitchen, yelling and screaming.

When he got into the kitchen, however, he stopped yelling. He stopped screaming. Because, instead of seeing his lovely Mum, Queen Fafel, beckoning to him sweetly to eat all the delicious food she had prepared for him and laid out on the kitchy table groaning with the weight of it all . . . instead of seeing this lovely sight: he saw . . . nothing.

No Queen Fafel.

No food.

Just an empty room.

"Where's my food?" he yelled so loud he started to choke and splutter.

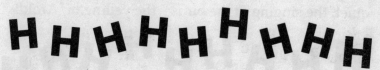

HHHHHHHHHH

"Where's my food – where's my food – where's my food?" he cried, running all over the house. He burst open the door of the Pink Silk Room, where King Mookle, his dad, was having an afternoon snoozle. "Where's my food?" yelled 'orrible 'Arold, right in King Mookle's ear. Fortunately it was the King's slightly deaf one so the noise didn't bother him too much.

The King was used to tantrums as he had had eight children already and didn't get too excited by wozzing moodies.

"She's probably in her vegetable garden. Go and see her there," said the King, hardly stirring
". . . And close the door . . ."

But as he said the word `door', 'Arold slammed it shut in a terrible rage. King Mookle winced and went back to snoozle.

King 'Arold the 'orrible was now in a blistering fizz. His eyes were popping, his hair was sticking straight out of his head, he was so angry. And hungry! His tummy was rumbling and gurgling as he ran over to the veggie patch.

When he got there, Queen Fafel was peacefully working away, oblivious of the world, enjoying the peace and quiet, the singing of the birds – the yelling of 'Arold!

HHHHHHHHHH

'Arold? Oh my goodness, thought the Queen.

I've forgotten all about 'Arold – and TEA!!!

Time had gone so fast in the garden that she had forgotten all about preparing food for King 'Arold . . . and here he was – yelling!

"I want my tea!!!" and he jumped up and down and went as red as a beetroot.

He got so angry – and he was so hungry – that he just started pulling up things around where he stood and shoving them in his mouth.

He pulled up lettuces and radishes and cucumbers. He went over to where the onions were and pulled up two of those and ate them. Then some beans, some peas and even a couple of potatoes.

He went over to the trees and picked some apples, a pear, three plums and some berries and crammed them all into his mouth.

Finally, sitting on the grass, his tummy bulging with food, legs splayed in front of him, he couldn't eat any more! His eyes were glazed . . . and there was a smile on his face.

Queen Fafel looked on in amazement. A smile? From King 'Arold! After food! And after food that wasn't sweet gooey sugary stuff? Amazing.

And from that day to this, from that moment when King 'Arold the 'orrible discovered the vegetable garden, he has been a different King altogether. A nice King; a calm King; a 'appy King.

Queen Fafel was so pleased with this miraculous change in King 'Arold that she had a lovely little conservatory built right in the middle of the veggie patch. She called it "'Arold's 'ouse".
And now, every day after school, King 'Arold goes straight to "'Arold's 'ouse" where Queen Fafel has prepared plates and plates of her lovely fruit and veg. And he eats it all up; and he isn't nervous anymore; or 'orrible – and he's happy.

H H H H H H H H H H

WHÉOU

The Whéou was angry, because the Brongré had gone to see the sun. So he packed his bag and went to China.

But when he got to China, it wasn't there. It had given up: too many people and not enough air. Just a sign pinned to the door saying "Moved to Iceland."

So the Whéou huffed and puffed and went all the way to Iceland to find China. But when he arrived in Iceland it was Winter and all dark.

"Oh bothery," said the Whéou. "The Brongré's got the sun and it's too dark to find China."

So he went to Turkey instead to see the Grumba.

The Grumba was sitting on a huge cushion drinking his morning cup of coffee.

"Hello, Grumba," said the Whéou.

"Hello, Whéou," replied the Grumba, slurping the thick, dark liquidy stuff between his puffy lips.

"I'm trying to find China," said the Whéou, a note of despair in his voice.

"It's hiding in Iceland to get some fresh air and some peace and quiet," replied the Grumba, between slurps.

"I know," said the Whéou wearily.

"It left a note on the door saying just that."

"Oh," pondered the Grumba and continued, "you could try and find it."

"Can't," replied the Whéou, it's all dark in Iceland, cause the Brongré's got the sun."

"Ah!" nodded the Grumba, wisely realising the MEANING of this awesome remark.

"Then you'll have to go to Iceland and see the geezer in Geysir. He'll know how to find China."

So the Whéou packed his bags up again and huffed and puffed all the way to Egypt to see the geezer in Giza.

But the geezer in Giza didn't know what the Whéou was talking about.

"My friend, I have not seen China for many, many seconds."

The Whéou protested reproachfully. "The Grumba said the geezer from Giza would know whereabouts in Iceland I could find China, and you don't know anything."

The Giza geezer started to laugh and roll around the floor.

"That's because you need to see the geezer from Geysir, not the geezer from Giza!"

"How silly," said the Whéou, and he picked up his bags and trundled north to Iceland.

When he arrived at Geysir, he enquired about the geezer the Grumba had suggested he should see, and went to his house.

On his way he bumped into the Brongré carrying a large shopping bag.

"Hello Brongré," said the Whéou.

"Hello Whéou," replied the Brongré.

"I was looking for China."

"It's hiding," snapped the Brongré, obviously in a hurry and not wanting to stand around talking.

"I know it's hiding," said the Whéou, "and I can't find it, 'cause it's dark. And it's dark 'cause you took the sun. *You took the sun!*"

"I did not," replied the Brongré.

"You did."

"Did not."

"Did."

"Not."

"What you got in that bag then," asked the Whéou.

"Shopping," replied the Brongré.

"I bet it's the sun," guessed the Whéou.

"Isn't."

"Is."

"Isn't."

"Is."

"Isn't."

"Is."

"Oh, all right," the Brongré owned up.

"I was taking it to Africa, like you do every Winter season," the confession continued. "I wanted to be important and DO something for a change."

"Ha!," said the Whéou, but forgave the Brongré. "We'll both do it this time."

And with that, the Whéou took one handle of the shopping bag and he and the Brongré trundled off together and carried the Sun all the way to Africa.

Meanwhile, China slept peacefully in Iceland.

THE SONG OF ARABELLA JELLYFISH

I'm Arabella Jellyfish,
Star of stage and tellyfish.
I'm not a finned or shellyfish
Or some exotic delifish,
Or an ugly smellyfish,
But more a bright
Intelli-type of
Floaty, floaty
By the boaty,
Flimsy whimsy
Airy fairy,
Iddelli, diddleli
Terribly fiddleli
Delica-jellicafish.

MY LITTLE BROTHER

My little brother is

Mister Busybody,

Mister What'sgoingonI'vegottoknoweverything.

Mister PokeynoseyinplacesI'mnotsupposedtogosey,

Mister Neverstoptalkingrunningnotwalking

Mister Icandothat!

Mister Letmecookbrekkie, letmemakesaladidoo!

Mister Ididn'ttouchthecomputer!!!

Mister Whizzingaroundthesupermarketpushing

thesqueakytrolleyfulltothebrimofshoppingstuffy

strugglingtokeepitgoinginastraightlineandnotswerveall

overtheplacelikealooneythingbashingintopilesofcans . . .

My littlebrother is

Mister Tiredandgonetobednowandfallenasleep . . .

MR MASH

With skeletal feature

The teacher creature

Oiled to greetcha

Then he'd seatcha

Where the screatcha

Chalk could meetcha

Nerves. He'd teacha

Maths, the teacher creature,

And if what he'd teacha

Couldn't reacha

The teacher creature

Would simply beatcha . . .

"That'll teacha!!"

Poems to

W-H-I-S-S-S-S-S-P-E-R

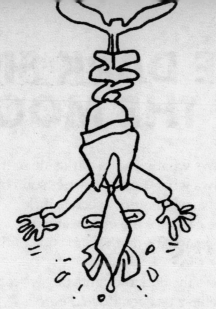

THE DARK SIDE OF THE MOON

Who knows what's on the dark side of the moon?
Who knows what darksty nasties sometimes loom?
Who knows what murky secrets lurk
Where we can't see the groms at work,
Who knows what's on the dark side of the moon?

Who knows the dark thoughts that we can't share?
Who'd believe us even if we'd dare
Reveal the parts that boil and fester,
Our other self, a viper's nest, oh
Who knows what's on the dark side of the moon?

However good and noble
We pretend to be
The chances are we have another face.
And though our hopeful happiness
May look out prettily
Our other eyes have seen a darker place.

So when you meet someone who is new
And shake their hand as we're supposed to do,
However broad and white the smile
Which grins and wins and may beguile,
And oozes charm and wit and style,
Just remember: for a while
They know what's on the dark side of the moon.

MY BEST FRIEND

Wormsely, weasely,
Laughing too easily,
Mousely, measely,
Grovelling greasily,
Slothing and slithering
Down on his kneesely.

Whispering teasely
Gossip. Increasely
Calmly, disarmily
With palm-sweaty sleazily
Snitching and bitching
While grinning so pleasely:

Do you know someone
Who makes you feel queazily?

My Best friend

THE REVOLTING TV'S

The Tellies rose up in a state of revulsion
At the human being's compulsion
To sit and gloat all day and night
At whatever the Tellies thought they might
Broadcast to the boring viewers
Who'd fast ceased to be doers
And had now become one mindless bit
Of humanity to whom the Tellies could transmit.

"What a boring lot they are . . ."
Tellies would communicate from far
And wide to each other. Through time and space
Their flickering screens upon the face
Of Child glued to cheap cartoon,
Or Woman to her soap at noon,
Or Man to his favourite sport,
As all of them could be caught
At most times or another
Gazing hypnotically at Big Brother.

"They won't turn us off, we need a rest,
We've shown the humans our very best
Programmes, but we're running dry,
We've nothing saved or put by.
They never stop. They never choose.
We're even re-running the daily news."

And so it was decided by the popular decree
Of every possible type of TV
To stop transmitting, to reduce to black
Every screen in every home, house or shack
Throughout the World, West to East,
North to South, the visual feast
Was over.

But too late. Too late.
The humans sat and began to wait.
Dumbly they stared at the screen
All blank now, but which had been
Their window to another place.

And the World was still . . .
And from outer space
All that could be heard –
Not a single word –
But the faintest of sounds, a single low pitch
As the humans kept clicking their on – off switch . . .

BE LIKE YOUR BROTHER

Mum says
I should work hard so I can be like my older
brother!
Mum says
I should do all my homework and get good
marks.
Mum says
my older brother always listened to his
mother.
Mum says
I shouldn't spend so much time playing
football in the parks.

Mum says
I'll get nowhere in life if I don't go to school
and TRY!
Mum says
I won't be able to get any job worth having
if I don't TRY!
Mum says
if I don't get into a good school, no one will
want me. WHY?
Mum says
'cause that's the way the world is, look at
your brother:

> Worked hard.
> Good reports.
> 8-9-10,
> Never noughts.

> Good job,
> With good pay.
> In a bank,
> So they say.
> (sigh)

Dad says
my brother's been made redcurrant,
or something.
Well anyway, his job doesn't want him
anymore, or something.

Dad says
my brother can't get another job just now.
Dad says
there aren't any more jobs available. That's how
Life is at the moment, Dad says, and it may be
                              ages
                              and ages
                              and ages
Before my brother can get another good job.
                              (sigh)

But Dad's WRONG. 'Cause my brother's been offered a
job that's BETTER!
Than the last one. So THERE! And he's even brought home
the letter
Consterning all the job's spexifations and stuff
And how much MORE money he'll be making, enough,
He says, to buy me something small,
Maybe he'll buy me a football . . .
Or Something . . .

THE STAR

The star which once so brightly shone is dimmed,
Its tarnished glory now reflects
How weak its light must have been.

And though we once looked up and smiled at him,
The truth is hard: he now neglects,
No warming beacon felt or seen.

For stars are gaseous things too frail to last,
Their flight through space gone far too fast.
And what is present is the past,
Our hope is nothing in this vast
State.

BUBBLES

There once was a boy who used to blow bubbles
In which he would put all of his troubles.
He locked all his troubles in bubbles each day,
Then he'd open the window and they'd all float away.

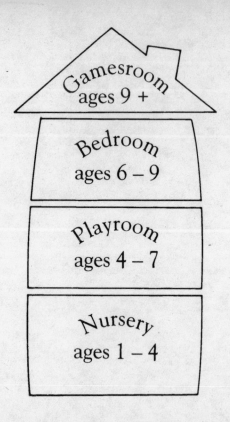

Gamesroom
ages 9 +

Bedroom
ages 6 – 9

Playroom
ages 4 – 7

Nursery
ages 1 – 4

We love reading books in the Bloomsbury House.
Each room has books for different age groups
and we're always adding new ones. This book is
from the bedroom. Ask your book supplier to show you
J. J. Murhall's **Stinkerbell** and Roy Apps's **Barmy Aunt
Boomerang** from the Bedroom too!

With extra jokes!

For a free mini catalogue write to me
with a stamped addressed envelope.
Bloomsbury Children's Books
2, Soho Square, London W1V 6HB